No Fair!

Kids Talk About Fairness

Written by
Nancy Loewen

Illustrated by
Omarr Wesley

Content Advisor: Lorraine O. Moore, Ph.D., Educational Psychology

Reading Advisor: Lauren A. Liang, M.A., Literacy Education, University of Minnesota

PICTURE WINDOW BOOKS
Minneapolis, Minnesota

Editor: Nadia Higgins
Designer: Thomas Emery
Page production: Picture Window Books
The illustrations in this book were prepared digitally.

Picture Window Books
5115 Excelsior Boulevard
Suite 232
Minneapolis, MN 55416
1-877-845-8392
www.picturewindowbooks.com

Printed in the United States of America.

Library of Congress Cataloging-in-Publication Data
Loewen, Nancy, 1964-
  No fair! : kids talk about fairness / written by Nancy Loewen ; illustrated by
Omarr Wesley.
     p. cm.
  Summary: Tina Truly's advice column answers questions from young people
about school and family situations that seem unfair. Includes bibliographical
references and index.
  ISBN 1-4048-0033-6 (library binding : alk. paper)
  1. Fairness—Juvenile literature. [1. Fairness. 2. Questions and answers.]
I. Wesley, Omarr, ill.
II. Title.
  BJ1533.F2 L64 2003
  179'.9—dc21
                                                            2002005889

To my children,
Louis and Helena–
always my best teachers

4

Hey, there! I'm Tina Truly. People call me T. Welcome to my advice column. Kids write to me about stuff that's bothering them, and I tell them what I think. This is going to be a blast!

FYI (that's "For Your Information"), I'm 13 years old and in the seventh grade at Meandering Middle School. I live with my dad and stepmom and big brother, Josh. Some people (like Josh) think I want to be an advice columnist because I like telling everyone else what to do. Well, maybe that's a teensy part of it. But mostly, I just like thinking things through. I like helping people. And I'm a total advice column addict myself—I'm the only kid I know who reads "Dear Abby" in the newspaper every single day.

Today's column is about fairness. You know, what's RIGHT? What's reasonable? What's not? And what can you do when a situation isn't fair?

So, hey, send in your letters. I'm ready!

Sincerely,

Tina Truly

Dear T. Truly:

The cafeteria lady yelled at me for starting a food fight. But I didn't do it! Sam did—I saw him fling those mashed potatoes myself. But whenever I go to lunch now, she always glares at me. What can I do?

Innocent

Dear Innocent:

That happened to me once, in the fourth grade. Only it wasn't about a food fight, it was about passing notes in class. I didn't do it—Marcy did—but my teacher didn't believe me. I felt awful.

My stepmom said I should talk to my teacher in private, so I did. The next day, I came in early from recess. I was sooooo nervous. But after we talked, I felt better. My teacher even said she was sorry for not believing me.

I think that's what you should do with the cafeteria lady. Tell her you want her to know that you didn't start that food fight. Use your best manners, and she'll be more likely to believe you. (It helps to practice what you're going to say in front of the mirror. That's what I did.) I bet she stops glaring at you. And if she still thinks you're a troublemaker—hey, at least you tried. You know inside that you're right.

One more word of advice: Don't sit anywhere near Sam. At least not when you're having mashed potatoes.

T. Truly

Dear T. Truly:

There's this girl in my class who is driving me crazy! She's Little Miss Perfect. She does great cartwheels and handstands and can jump rope forever without missing a step. I wish I could be her for just one day.

Just Your Average Kid

Dear Average Kid:

Every class has a kid who seems to get all the breaks. In my class it's Zoe. She took first place at the science fair AND won a trophy in horseback riding, all in one day!

A while ago, Zoe was really driving me nuts. We were getting ready for the school carnival. She sold twice as many tickets as I did. And her idea for a Make-a-Kite Booth beat out my idea for a Bobbing-for-Pickles Booth. But you know what? I ended up having a great time. I got to run the Spelling Bee, and I made everybody laugh by reading the words with a snooty accent. Once I got on a roll with that, I didn't think about Zoe a bit.

My dad says that being jealous is a waste of time. He says, "Don't worry about other people—just do what you want to do." Little Miss Perfect could jump rope around the whole world, but that doesn't make YOU less special.

T. Truly

Dear T.:

My parents love my big brother more than me. He gets
to stay up later. He gets a bigger allowance. He's got a
scooter and his very own CD player. It's just not fair!

Little Brother

Dear Little Brother:

I know what you mean. I feel that way sometimes about my older brother, too. Whenever I get into a snit about all the things Josh gets to do, my dad and stepmom say, "Your turn will come." I *hate* it when they say that! But, sometimes it kind of makes sense. Like, when I was younger, I counted the years, the months, and the weeks until I was old enough to go to Camp Cannaworms like Josh did. I finally got to go last year. My turn DID come. (Camp Cannaworms was fun, but boy, I never knew mosquitoes could get that big.)

And another thing. I bet your parents don't really love your brother more. Love doesn't have anything to do with presents or privileges—my stepmom told me that once. Josh can do more things than I can, but that doesn't mean my parents love him more. Would my dad give me all his red jelly beans if he didn't love me?

I bet if you think about it, you'll come up with lots of ways your parents show you that they love you. My advice is, focus on those things, and focus on what you CAN do. You'll feel a lot better.

T. Truly

14

Dear T.:

My mom says I have to go to bed at 8:00. Lots of my friends get to stay up until 9:00—and my best friend, Tyrone, can go to bed whenever he wants. I tell my mom that only babies go to bed at 8:00, but she doesn't care. What can I do?

Not Sleepy in Seattle

Dear Not Sleepy:

Well, not all babies go to sleep that early. My friend Paul has a baby sister who bawls her head off every night until midnight. He says he'd give his big toe for one good night's sleep. I think he really means it.

Your question definitely calls for my two-step plan. I call the first step, "Covering Your Bases." First, think about what your mom's going to say. She's probably going to come at you with all kinds of reasons why you need an early bedtime. Like, do you get crabby if you don't get enough sleep? Are you hard to wake up in the morning? Do you drag your feet at school? You need to think about your answers.

After you have your answers all figured out, then you can move on to Step Two. I call this, "Laying It on the Table." Pick a time when your mom isn't busy. Calmly tell her what you want, and why. No whining! (Trust me, whining *never* works.) Give her some specific ideas to work with. Like, maybe you could go to bed at 8:30 for a week to see how it goes. Or maybe you could stay up later on the weekends.

I can't guarantee instant results, but my two-step plan has a very high success rate. It took eight months and three sessions of "Laying It on the Table," but I was finally allowed to start babysitting the neighborhood kids. And guess what I got on my last birthday? Tickets to the Bobblehead Boys concert! So hang in there, Not Sleepy.

T. Truly

Dear T. Truly:

My dad lost his job and hasn't been able to find another one. Now I can't go to karate lessons anymore. And our summer vacation has been canceled. My life is ruined!

In the Dumps

Dear In the Dumps:

That's tough. For sure. My friend Dana went through something like that when her mom was out of work. At first Dana complained a lot, but that phase didn't last too long. She said she felt sorry for her mom—it wasn't like her mom lost her job on purpose or anything. Her family tried really hard to save money. Like, they bought frozen pizza at the grocery store instead of having pizza delivered, and they didn't get a lot of presents at Christmas—things like that. Dana said that some of it was okay, though. They played lots of games and flew kites and had picnics in parks all over town.

Dana's mom has a great new job now, so things worked out. But Dana says she sometimes misses those days when she got to spend so much time with her mom.

I hope your dad finds a job soon. In the meantime, let your dad know that you're behind him 100 percent. And if you get discouraged, keep telling yourself: "I'm strong! I can handle this!"

T. Truly

Dear Tina:

My brother went to six parties last month. Now I've been invited to a party, but my dad says no. Instead, I have to go to my grandparents' stupid wedding anniversary. How can I get my dad to change his mind?

Party Pooper

Dear Party Pooper:

Hmmmmm. This is a difficult case. I doubt that even my two-step plan would work in these circumstances. Nope, this case clearly calls for Step Three. (I only use it in emergencies.) It's called "Making the Best of a Bad Situation."

Going to the anniversary instead of the birthday party—that's a done deal. It's just the way things worked out this time. But whatever you do, don't go there and act all grumpy the whole time. That will just make your grandparents give you hurt looks. Your parents will get seriously mad at you, and your brother will win the "best kid" title.

You need to put a positive spin on this and make it as much fun as you can. You're sure to get cake, right? Will your cousins be there? You might even end up impressing your dad with your "mature attitude." Who knows where that could lead?

Good luck, Party Pooper!

T. Truly

21

Dear T. Truly:

Why does my teacher call on me when I don't know the answer? Why does the phone ring during the best part of a TV show? Why does bread fall on the floor with the jelly side down?

Just Wondering

Dear Just Wondering:

I've got one for you. Why does the school cafeteria always serve sauerkraut on math-test days? It's all part of something called Murphy's Law. "Anything that can go wrong WILL go wrong"—that's it in a nutshell. Grown-ups blame Murphy's Law when they lock their keys in the car or when their kids get out the finger paints right before company comes (I'm not naming any names here).

But is Murphy's Law really true, or is it just some crazy idea? Hmmm. This could make a really neat experiment. You could keep track of all the times the phone rings and compare that to the number of times you're at a good part in a TV show. Drop bread on the floor and see how many times it lands jelly side down. (Be sure to have lots of newspaper on the floor, or you'll really be in a jam!)

Make sure to let me know what your results are. You might be on the brink of a major scientific discovery!

T. Truly

Dear T. Truly:

My mom says I carry the weight of the world on my shoulders. I keep thinking about all the ways life isn't fair. Like, how so many people don't have enough food or clean water. Or how people get sick or have bad accidents. Or don't get jobs just because of their race. Then there are disasters like earthquakes and hurricanes. Can you help me sort this out?

Discouraged in Denver

Well, everyone, that's it for today's questions. Thanks for writing! Keep reading for a fun quiz and more.

Dear Discouraged:

I know what you mean. Fairness is hard to figure. A tornado came through our town last summer. One house was completely destroyed, while the one next door wasn't damaged at all. How fair was that?

As my big brother would say, this is a "cosmic" question. It's a biggie. People have been asking these questions since the beginning of time, and no one has come up with an answer yet.

The thing is, life ISN'T fair. That's not the way it's set up. Some things, like the tornado, we just have to accept. But that doesn't mean we have to give in to wimphood! There are lots of things we can do to help turn bad stuff around. Maybe not on a big scale, like getting rid of world hunger. But in smaller ways, we can all make the world a better place. Definitely!

Maybe you could pick out one thing that really bothers you and figure out a way to take action. Like, if you're worried about people going hungry, ask your parents if your family could volunteer at a soup kitchen. I know a kid named Frances who got her whole neighborhood to give toys and clothes to an orphanage in Russia. She was really proud of that. I'll bet doing something like that would help you feel better, too.

Let me know what you decide to do.

T. Truly

It's Quiz Time!

Here's a quiz I wrote. Don't worry. It's *so* much more fun than the ones you take in school.

1. If your brother gets something you don't, you should:

    A. put a stinky piece of cheese under his bed.
    B. forget about it and pay attention to the good things in your life.
    C. stop talking to everyone but the dog.

2. If you don't agree with the house rules, the best plan is to:

    A. go live with your best friend's family.
    B. talk it over with your parents, but realize that you might not get your way.
    C. break the rules every chance you get until everyone in the family goes bonkers.

3. To be jealous means:

    A. that you want what someone else has.
    B. that you like to eat jelly.
    C. that you absolutely adore Jell-O.

4. What's the problem with being jealous?

    A. It keeps you from seeing how terrific YOU are.
    B. It makes you burp.
    C. Within 48 hours of feeling jealous, you'll start turning into a green-eyed monster.

5. The best thing to do when you're bummed out about something is to:

    A. stamp your feet until the house shakes.
    B. deal with it and move on.
    C. mope around for five days straight.

6. **If you get blamed for something you didn't do, you should:**

   A. take out an ad in the newspaper defending yourself.
   B. start an embarrassing rumor about the person who blamed you.
   C. stand up for yourself, without being mean about it.

7. **According to my two-step plan, "Covering Your Bases" means:**

   A. kicking sand all over the bases in the softball field.
   B. thinking about the problems that might come up and figuring out a way around them.
   C. wearing a towel when you get out of the tub.

8. **"Laying It on the Table" means:**

   A. telling someone exactly how you feel.
   B. setting the table for supper.
   C. that it's time for someone to deal the cards.

9. **If one of your parents loses a job, you should:**

   A. go for the grungy look—dress in rags and stop washing your face.
   B. rob a lemonade stand.
   C. try to be patient and encouraging and hopeful.

10. **Murphy's Law:**

    A. is an ancient scientific theory.
    B. is on TV on Tuesday nights at 8:00 P.M. (Eastern/Pacific Time).
    C. is an expression people use when little things go wrong.

Answer Key:

1-B, 2-B, 3-A, 4-A, 5-B, 6-C, 7-B, 8-A, 9-C, 10-C

From My Personal Hero File: Susan B. Anthony

To my readers:

A little while ago, I did a report on Susan B. Anthony for history class. She's someone who devoted her whole LIFE to the idea of fairness. Here are some of the things I learned.

Susan B. Anthony was one of the people who started the women's suffrage movement. *Suffrage* means to vote. See, until 1920, women in the U.S. couldn't even vote—just because they were women! Can you imagine that?

Susan B. Anthony was born in 1820 in Massachusetts. She was from a Quaker family. Quakers didn't believe in war or slavery, and they thought men and women should be treated equally. So that's where Susan got a lot of her ideas.

Susan started out as a teacher, but she didn't think it was fair that she was paid one-fifth as much as the teachers who were men. She protested—and was fired from her job. After that she got a better job as the principal at a girls' school. But she left that job after 10 years in order to spend more time on social causes—ESPECIALLY getting women the right to vote. She organized meetings and wrote lots of papers. She spoke before Congress every single year from 1869 to 1906. In 1872 she managed to cast her vote in a presidential election, but later she was arrested and fined $100. (She refused to pay it, though, and eventually was left alone.)

Susan B. Anthony died in 1906. She was really old—86! Her last words spoken in public were "Failure is impossible." (Don't you just love how determined she was?) When she died, only four states let women vote. But thanks to Susan and lots of other determined people, the suffrage movement was getting stronger. And in 1920, Congress adopted the 19th Amendment. It gives women all through the United States the right to vote. Pretty awesome, huh?

Words to Know

Check out this list of cool words and expressions I put together. You can use it to help you remember all the stuff we talked about.

advice column—a feature in magazines and newspapers (and in this case, a book). People write in with questions, and some really smart person called a columnist writes back with answers.

cosmic question—a big question about life, the universe, and everything. What is the meaning of life? What is eternity? Are aliens real? Things like that.

fairness—Even after doing this column, it's hard to put this idea into words! To be fair is to be reasonable ... just ... respectful. To consider what's right, and do the right thing.

food fight—Oh, come on. Don't pretend you don't know this one!

Making the Best of a Bad Situation—trying to relax and have fun even if the situation isn't what you wanted

manners—polite behavior. Saying please and thank you, not interrupting, making eye contact, not eating your tuna casserole with your fingers—all of that.

mature attitude—If you have a mature attitude, it means you're acting like a grown-up: being responsible, considerate, patient, and so on. (Hey, not even grown-ups act that way ALL the time.)

positive spin—This one's very closely related to "Making the Best of a Bad Situation." Basically, putting a positive spin on something means looking for the good and trying not to let the bad stuff get to you.

privilege—a benefit or an advantage that goes beyond the basics. Here's an example: Having some free time in the summer is basic. Going to Camp Cannaworms (even with all the mosquitoes) falls into the privilege category.

sauerkraut—old cabbage that's been sitting in its own juices for a long time. Some people actually eat it!

snit—a fit of anger about something that's not a big deal

social causes—People dream about how they want their world to be a better place. Like, wouldn't it be great if everyone had enough food to eat, or if everyone was treated the same no matter how they looked? The dreams turn into social causes when enough people start working together to make those dreams come true.

31

To Learn More

At the Library

Ketteman, Helen. *Mama's Way*. New York: Dial Books for Young Readers, 2001.

Kline, Suzy. *Molly Gets Mad*. New York: Putnam's, 2001.

Krudop, Walter Lyon. *The Man Who Caught Fish*. New York: Farrar, Straus & Giroux, 2000.

Levete, Sarah. *Being Jealous*. Brookfield, Conn.: Copper Beech Books, 1999.

Porter, Connie Rose. *Addy's Little Brother*. Middleton, Wis.: Pleasant Publications, 2000.

Fact Hound

Fact Hound offers a safe, fun way to find Web sites related to this book. All of the sites on Fact Hound have been researched by our staff. *http://www.facthound.com*

1. Visit the Fact Hound home page.
2. Enter a search word related to this book, or type in this special code: 1404800336.
3. Click the FETCH IT button.

Your trusty Fact Hound will fetch the best sites for you!

Index